MW01196935

YOUR PART IN THE

~ by

VALIANT THOR AND MICHAEL X.BARTON

* * * *

This is an Educational and Inspir-
ational Course of Study...especially
written and intended for NEW AGE Individuals everywhere. The following
Seven Sections are contained herein:

1. "THE MASTER PLAN IS KNOWN"

2. "WHY THE KNOWERS NEED YOU"

3. "YOUR SPECIAL TASK NOW"

4. "AID FROM OUTER SPACE"

5. "ROCK WILL TURN TO GOLD"

6. "WHAT OTHERS ARE DOING"

7. "YOUR THREE GOLDEN KEYS"

* * * * *

Statements in this Course are based
on Scientific and Super-Sensory Find-
ings.   No claim is made as to what
the information cited may do in any
given case and the Publishers assume
no obligation for opinions expressed
or implied herein by the author.

SBN-13: 978-1979601085
ISBN-10: 1979601089

PRINTING HISTORY
New Age Press edition published 1960
Saucerian Press edition published 1982
New Saucerian Press edition published 2018

©2018 New Saucerian, LLC

INTRODUCTION

Once again, dear New Age Friend, it is my great joy to be with you -- heart and spirit -- in the pages of this vital book.

Now our task -- yours and mine -- is to find our part in the Great Cosmic Plan of the Supreme Head of this Universe..GOD.

Where we have been vague or uncertain about our individual role before..now we must become certain. We must gain a vision --crystal clear--of our special activity.

After you have read this book and taken the "NEW AGE PLEDGE" voluntarily, you become a true "NEW AGER"...dedicated to THE PLAN.

Although we writers try, no man can put THE PLAN into any fixed or "static" set of dogmatic words. THE PLAN is too big for that. It is Cosmic in scope and ever expanding to encompass every level of life.

THE PLAN includes your highest welfare and unlimited progress, physically, mentally and spiritually. It touches all humanity.

This book was written with my heart as well as my hand. For even as I wrote, I was given to know and understand that THE PLAN itself is purest LOVE in expression.

I am confident in my belief that your part in The Plan is a magnificently important one. Do your part joyously, however humble or insignificant it may seem to be at the time, and the result will not be in the least insignificant.

You, I and NEW AGERS everywhere will release Mankind into a higher freedom than it has ever known on Planet Shan!

Your NEW-AGE Companion,

MICHAEL X

PREFACE

So vast is this subject that I can only whet your appetite. The Invisible Government of our section of the universe rules over 144,000 planets. Our own solar system revolves about a central sun and is made up of 12 planets (of which 9 are known).

Since God needs spiritual helpers at all levels, each planet has a spiritual ruler - in your case, Jesus the Christ, known as Sananda on the Solar Board. His predecessor was Sanat Kumara, who with others from Venus, came to save Earth, which was populated by less evolved souls from other planets (who could not adjust on their home planets).

Their mission will end when the Aquarian Age draws to a close. A council of 24 elders and 12 representatives (one for each planet) heads your solar system. These Masters who hold offices in the spiritual government have all surmounted the tests of Lower Self, though it may have taken them many lifetimes. Now they can point the way for us to do the same.

Each is a specialist in one of seven fields of work. These include politics, religion, education, science, philosophy, psychology, and economics. They are constantly working for World BETTERMENT. But in doing this, the Law of Free Will is never violated - nobody is coerced. They seek to improve relationships between races and groups, using cooperation and goodwill. Results of their work can be seen in more interrelation and communication worldwide.

To assist the Council Masters, a group called World Servers was established 50 years ago. They are the "elect* who carry out the Great Plan. Their objective is to help humanity to evolve spiritually through sacrifice, love, joy, and daily meditation. The Plan Objective is to increase love and light, and to release the Divine Will in man.

Goals of the Great Plan include preparation for the reappearance of the Christ, cleansing Earth, decreasing our workload, the liberation of women and people of color, development of one single language, a new economic system, affordable advanced medicine, and a truly democratic world government.

We could go on to the functions and offices of the hierarchy, but enough has been said to make you realize the profound effect of the hierarchy commonly called "angels" in our lives. PRAISE GOD FOR THESE DIVINE HELPERS IN OUR TIME OF NEED!

I thank Michael X. for his help in laying out our Plan to you, dear reader. I leave no "return address,* nor do you need one. I know each of you by name, and your innermost thoughts. You address me through your hearts and spirits on an ongoing basis. Adoni Vasu...

-Valiant Thor

YOUR PART IN THE GREAT PLAN

Part 1

The Master Plan is Known

I am hungry. All around me I see millions of other hungry persons. I see you among those in my own intimate circle of friends, and I see that you are hungry also.

YES! We are all hungry... but not for bread. For a long time now we've had a sufficiency of bread. Now we want to know -- really know -- what life is all about. What our purpose is and how we may fulfill it.

Last night I sat in front of my television set, watching the action on the TV screen. I turned to the first channel and saw a band of cowboys pursuing Indians across the plains. For some reason I wasn't interested. I turned to another channel.

Bang! Bang! Bang! Criminals were shooting it out with the police and I don't know who was getting the worst of it. So I switched to the next channel. I'm sorry I did.

A violent fist fight was going on before my eyes. It was all taking place upon a balcony of some house. Wow! One man hit the other man such a solid blow that the railing of the balcony gave way and down the victim crashed to the courtyard below. How brutal can these shows get? And why?

Naturally, I switched to a more peaceable, educational type of show. Violence hadn't fed my inner hunger, perhaps the non-violent programs would. I watched quietly.

Occasionally I could "read between the lines" of the television program and observe one vital thing. Some of the television writers are sensing the New Age spirit. A few exciting, inspiring glimpses of deeper truths are being shows to the public. Man is reaching for new standards!

Desperately now, humanity everywhere is searching. It is simply a search for a better set of values for human life, a way of life more abundant if you will, that goes beyond the eat, work, escape and sleep routine of ordinary living.

There must be some Plan, some higher purpose for humanity. Some secret pattern that, whether we realize it consciously or not, is steadily working for human good.

Why has The Plan, if one exists, escaped us so long?

Well, could be we've been so busily occupied in other matters that we've been overlooking the most important theme of all. The Big Plan and its Originator and our special part in that Plan.

Secretly, The Plan -- The Master Plan -- has been recognized by quite a few of the world's religions. There have always been secret teachings down through the ages, that were given to the sincere searchers and hidden from those who had only a selfish motive, profaning the truth.

So The Great Plan has long been concealed from the great masses of humanity. But times have changed. We are now -- you and I and all mankind -- living in the Last Days of an old cycle. And at the ending of every great Age things are revealed to us that previously have been kept hidden.

"There is nothing hidden that shall not be revealed", and that is the simple reason I am writing this book. I intend to -- with your help and the aid of the Great Ones who may write through me -- shout the Truth from the house-tops! Are you with me? Good!! Then here we go!

God is the Originator of The Great Cosmic Plan. It is His Plan for Man. And of course it includes all of His creation, the Humans, the animals, the plants, minerals, planets and stars. All of the higher and all of the lower kingdoms of life are included within the "blueprint".

Some people -- we call them atheists -- have tried to eliminate the basic idea of God from their thinking. I've talked to some of them and they tell me they just don't believe in God. So I smile at them and say:

"You may not believe in God, but God believes in you!"

None of us would be here if some Supreme Intelligence wasn't running the show and giving us life. Every brilliant scientist who has allowed himself time to think on this matter knows there is a God. And God certainly must have a good and desirable Destiny in mind for His Universes and their inhabitants. You and I and the teeming millions of other human beings are not on this planet merely to eat, sleep and work our lives away. Heaven forbid! The Plan is a lot bigger than that!

It is actually a gigantic Plan. And it is a good Plan for the simple reason that its creator is good. And since the Intelligence behind the Plan is supremely wise, we can appreciate at once the fact that it must be a wise Plan.... above mere human meddling.

The Plan is one of spiritual upliftment. We are each of us essentially spiritual beings. Unhappily, our policy of pursuing the "mixed-up" matters of our physical plane existence has gotten us deeply immersed in matter. I speak now more of the masses of humanity, not of you nor of other New Age individuals who are now on the Upward Path.

Remember that old coat, or that old suit of yours that you've worn for so long you are tired of it? Notice how you ignore it now. It most likely hasn't been out of your closet in a "month of Sundays". Why not?

Because you are ready to don a new garment, enjoy the new and get rid of the old. Just imagine how happy you'll feel all decked out in a brand new coat or suit!

That is exactly how you will be feeling soon. All of us are now living at the end of a major cycle of Time. It is the end of an Age. The Bible refers to this period as THE LATTER DAYS. But a new Age, the Golden Age, is rapidly approaching. In contrast to the present Age in which physical force and materiality has been King, the coming Golden Age will place Cosmic Love and Spirituality upon the throne.

This "Golden Age" or Time of Spirituality on earth, is not merely some human being's "pipedream". It is very real. And it is THE BIG FINALE of a realistic pattern or "Great Cosmic Plan" that is shaping the destiny of this world.

The Big Plan is known. Has been known to certain of Earth's adepts, initiates and prophets for some time now. Of course, details are continually being added as greater revelations come through from higher planes to the earth's plane. Make no mistake about it, the "Golden Millenium" of World Peace is in The Plan!

Not only the Master Jesus, but at least seven prophets predicted the coming Time of World Peace and Spirituality.

Plutarch, in his book, "Isis and Osiris" gives the following Prophecy of the Magi (one of the high orders of wise prophets.)

"It is the opinion and belief of the majority of the most ancient sages...that there will come a fated and pre-destined time when the earth will be completely leveled, united and equal. There will be but one mode of life and but one form of government (Theocracy or God-enlightened leader-ship) among mankind who will all speak one language and will live happily."

Picture it now with me, my friend. Beauty, peace, joy and the harmony of an abundant life. Former limitations of the Earth such as ignorance and disease banished forever from this sphere. The Kingdom of Heaven (Harmony and Truth) manifesting here on this planet, now and for a thousand years! Just imagine no prisons, because the man of good-will has no evil or criminal intent! No hospitals, because every man, woman and child would have come into harmony with all of the laws of Nature! No dissensions, "strikes", or poverty!

The Golden Age is coming. But, let us be practical. We have to finish living out the present closing Age in which we find ourselves, here and now. What is happening now?

Unpleasant things. Most of the things you hear about now -- and until the close of the 20th Century -- aren't very encouraging. Earthquakes, hurricanes galore, floods, etc. My next door neighbor -- a kindly old gentleman past 80 years -- told me recently in a tone of much concern, "I've never seen so much general confusion and unrest in the world as I see today! You just don't realize how awful it is!" And, being inclined toward optimism, perhaps I don't realize its awfulness; but I do certainly agree that it's there, dont you?

And the cause of it? Those who have studied "Solar Cycles" believe that the Solar System you and I live in is now receiving a greater vibratory stimulation. So too, do the scientists recognize it in the form of Cosmic Light bom-bardment from outer space. It is a positive stimulation and is coming from a larger Central Sun called Vela, around which our Sun and its planets are orbiting.

For some 7,000 years we (our Sun with its planets) have been receding from this Central Sun Vela in our orbit. But now, at the close of a great cycle of 7,200 years, our Solar System is approaching nearer to Vela. As it gets nearer, our Sun and Earth are more and more "quickened" in vibration by this more powerful influence which is faster, stronger, more "upsetting", and all of us are reacting one way or the other.

YOUR PART IN THE GREAT PLAN

Part 2

Why The Knowers Need You

New Age individuals who understand much more about The Great Plan -- about what is happening now within our Solar System, and WHY it is happening -- are called thruout this book, "Knowers of The Plan", or The Knowers". Let us briefly summarize what they know.

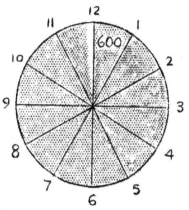

1. Humanity on planet Earth is now in process of evolving to a much higher condition than before. Eternal progress is the big rule, not only for human beings, but for all created forms in the Universe. Our Solar System, with the Earth and the other planets, is being perfected.

2. The Great Plan is geared in a simple way to a little-known but very perfect measure of time. This measure of time is computed by the movements of our Solar Sun, in relation to our Moon. It is called a Luni-Solar Year, or Moon-Sun Conjunction.

This Basic Period covers exactly 600 years. According to the great astronomer Cassini, it is the most perfect of periods. When a new moon takes place in any part of the heavens, it takes exactly 600 years to the second, for it to "conjunct" the Sun. That is, to appear under the same precise conditions...the sun, moon and stars being precisely in their same relative positions to one another.

The ancients called this 600 year period the "Naros". They discovered that it required a total of TWELVE such conjunctions of the Sun and Moon -- exactly 7,200 years -- for our Solar System and its planets to complete a single "orbital swing" around Vela. (Vela, being but one "Central sun" of many in our galaxy which revolve around the Great Central Sun at the hub of the Milky Way Galaxy.) This 7,200 year Cycle is the "Naronic Cycle".

Great Initiates such as Jesus and Pythagoras knew all about this Naronic Cycle. They knew that at the end of each 7,200 years our Solar Sun and Planets begin to approach much closer to Vela. Powerful energy vibrations from Vela then begin to influence our Solar System, causing all expressions of life upon our Sun and its planets to evolve into a higher -- more positive expression! This leads into the Golden Age!

I wish to call your attention now to the diagram just below. It depicts Vela and the "egg-shaped" orbit which our Solar System follows in making the swing around Vela.

Notice particularly that there are 12 divisions of time -- 600 year periods -- before the close of a Naronic Cycle. Jesus sent forth twelve apostles to commemorate this exceedingly important measure of time.

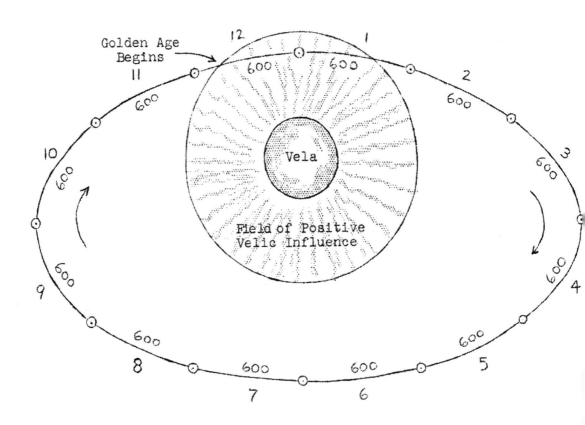

3. (The Knowers are informed that) During the twelve periods of the Naronic Cycle comprising 7,200 years, there appear Ten Messengers, or Messiahs. One Messenger every 720 years, comes to direct Mankind in his spiritual unfoldment. Hindu religion teaches that the Naronic Cycle is marked by the appearance of 10 Spiritual Teachers. And, in the land of Egypt, a most revealing practice was followed by the old Egyptian Priests. Whenever a King died, the priests at once

placed ten (10) crowns upon the coffin of the ruler. Each crown bore the symbolic figure of a serpent, the sign of the Messengers (who were wise in spiritual things) into whose keeping the soul of the King was entrusted.

4.   The Master Teacher Jesus appeared during the ninth (9th) period of the Naronic Cycle. We do not know for sure which one of the 600 years in his cycle was the one he was born in. But counting 600 X 9 = 5400. Subtracting 5400 from 7200 = 1800. This is the reason why, since the year 1800, the religious world has expected the end of the Age. (Not the end of the World. This will never be, as the world has a destiny to fulfill. Real meaning is the end of a Naronic Cycle or Age.)

The Tenth Messenger is due at any time now, and may even be here at this moment. Since we don't know which of the 600 years is the one in which Jesus was born, we can safely add 200 years to 1800. This would bring us to the turn of the century or the year 2000.

With the Tenth Messenger due now, the Knowers are firm in their conviction that THIS IS THE END OF AN AGE.

5.   The "Knowers" tell us that The Tenth Messenger will embody the attributes of Number 10, the Holy Spirit, or feminine polarity of God. Keynote of this is LOVE.

6.   Earth will undergo big changes. Land changes, political changes, religious changes, economic and social changes. These are the "Signs of the Times" or "Marks of the Age". As planet Earth comes under more intense stimulation of the big Central Sun Vela, humanity here will see unusual conditions.

The next 5-15 years will see many land changes, all intended to cleanse certain areas of this planet in preparation for the Golden Era. The outer condition as far as Mankind on earth is concerned, will be one of world unrest.

The Knowers assure us that we are not to fear these changes, but understand and welcome them! They are heralding the birthing of an earth beautiful beyond our dreams!

7.   A Swing from Material to Spiritual Values. Our world and its people, so long dedicated to the "worship of Material Success", will increasingly awaken to a new realization of true values. Old standards and values will become meaningless. Contrast between those who take their stand on the CAUSE SIDE (Spirit) and EFFECT SIDE (Matter) will sharpen.

8. Man must be prepared for Golden Age expression!
Here is where you, I, and all other NEW AGERS are needed by
the "Knowers" of The Plan. Planet Earth must be spiritually
prepared for a major rise in consciousness. Limited human
awareness will give way to Christ-Awareness. (God in Man) In
other words, we are to help others get the COSMIC viewpoint!

The Cosmic Viewpoint is big and unlimited. It is Life,
Love and Light acting as God's will in the universe to unite
men on planet Earth (and on all worlds) in right relationship
and right action: 1. Love God. 2. Love one another.

Since God is Light, Love and Life, and as God is in
each one of us, our job is to express Light, Love, Life. We
do this by "letting our Light shine"--loving one another;
living more spiritually and showing others how to do the same.
By doing this, we are uplifting the hearts and souls of those
around us, and preparing them for THE PLAN.

9. Interplanetary Confederation! Appearance of UFO's
or Spacecraft in our skies are Signs. They are part of the
"Space Phase" of this whole Program. Mankind on earth must
be educated and awakened to what is happening -- namely this:
A Spiritual Upliftment is beginning to take place within our
Solar System. Why? Because God is "expressing" Life, Love
and Light to cause all worlds to grow, to EVOLVE. Planet
Earth evolves under our Solar Sun. Our Solar System evolves
under the influence of Central Sun Vela. And Vela is also
evolving in the Universe. Progress cannot be impeded!

Let us continue. The United States of America has been
under spiritual guidance since its beginning. It will --
as the vibrations from Vela increase -- take the lead in
forming a Confederation of Nations on this planet. Then, if
all goes well and each one does his part in The Plan, our
Government will take the lid off the UFO "mystery" and ack-
nowledge SPACE VISITORS. Then our planet will join the Confederation of Planets that even now exists in our Solar System.

10. Everyone shares in Plan's Success. This whole tremendous Program for the upliftment of planet Earth and all
its humanity into a new and higher state of being -- is one
in which all Mankind shares. You and I and all men and women
of Good-will on Earth can aid the Plan, actually hasten it,
by consciously cooperating with it now. We can -- and thous-
ands of us now are -- sharing in the working out of the Great
Plan on all levels; mental, physical and spiritual. By ful-
filling our special roles vigorously, joyously, we are helping to lift the Earth from Darkness into LIGHT.

YOUR PART IN THE GREAT PLAN

Part 3

Your Special Task Now

The big question in your mind is, "Where exactly do I fit into the Great Plan? I want to serve to the best of my ability. But what do I do? And...how do I do it?

"EACH ONE REACH ONE"

You have a Special Role to play in this Great Plan. But before you can play it you must first know just what your part is.

Maybe you're lucky enough to have discovered it and to be living it now, but in case you have not yet become aware that you do have a part in the great scheme of the creator, take my word for it, you have.

What that part is you can truly know only from within yourself. I know what my part is, but I haven't the slightest idea as to what you are best able to do. However I do know this: Sure as you're born, God designed you to fit "as a piece of priceless mosaic" into His Great Cosmic Plan and in a manner that is uniquely your own. It's your task to find out how you may best serve The Plan in practical, positive ways.

I can also suggest how you may go about finding out. Seek the answer in receptive silence. Go for a long walk by yourself and while you are walking, ask yourself, your higher self, to tell you exactly what your Special Role is now, in the mighty Cosmic Drama now unfolding before you.

If you are dead serious about this, and "ask" in a deeply sincere and earnest way, you'll receive an answer. I guarantee it will be revealed to you from within. You will be given an inner "lead" or a sign, or a definite picture of your special "Assignment". It might be to do some speaking before a group, or express yourself through writing articles or books. It might be to serve on the Committee of some New Age Club. Then again, it might be to do just whatever you are doing more perfectly. Or to "speak a word in season to them that are weary", for that in itself, if the word is right is God's work. A woman I know was led to those very words in the Bible, as her part in The Plan.

I know of several persons who couldn't seem to find their "niche" in The Plan. Those good souls -- Genuine New Agers -- came to one of my public meetings one evening. I was teaching a Class at the time and during this class I gave a special technique to the students. I call it the "New Age Light Technique". You perform it as follows:

THE NEW AGE LIGHT TECHNIQUE

Step 1. Breathe deeply several times.

Step 2. Raise arms toward the Sun. If the Solar Sun has gone below the horizon, visualize clearly a large and brilliant Sun in the sky above you. Close your eyes while visualizing. Notice how your hands are tingling. Universal Energy is entering your body via your fingertips.

Step 3. Mentally draw Power into you by saying quietly (or audibly if with a group) "I am Life, I am Light, I am Love!" Repeat each affirmation exactly three times.

Step 4. Now slowly lower your arms and close hands to prevent any "leakage" of Cosmic Energy from your body. Do not open the hands for several minutes. If you should now desire to project the Power to others as a healing force, or to assist in re-energizing them, practice Step 5.

Step 5. Extend both arms straight in front of you and fill your lungs slowly with good, fresh air. If you know the exact locality where the one lives who is to receive the Light, point your hands in that direction.

If you do not know the exact direction, spread your fingers fanwise and will the Cosmic Energy or Light to instantly travel to the person whom you wish to receive it.

* * * * *

To make a long story short, the ones who couldn't seem to find their Special Role in The Great Plan, took a great interest in this "NEW AGE LIGHT TECHNIQUE". They began to put the Technique to use at once by indrawing Cosmic Light daily and sending it out to heal and uplift their friends.

"I've found my 'niche' at last, Michael X!" said one happy woman to me. "It's sending out the Light to others!"

Good idea! Bless others and you yourself find blessing. Lift and be lifted is a law of life that works. I am sure this activity of sending out the Light to others is a noble work. It's a much needed work. It is in line with the Great

Divine Plan. It may be, of course, only a small portion of what you will do for others in the thrilling days or years ahead. For you will be expressing yourself more and more in line with The Great Plan. Your major role will become clearer day by day. And here is a valuable pointer.

Practice this TECHNIQUE OF LIGHT for 3 minutes every day from now on. It will help your mind to become quickened, keen and alert. And what does that mean to you? It means a much clearer, freer, unobstructed channel will be established between you and your "Higher Self". That means you'll get answers to your daily problems more quickly and easily.

You will know what your special part in The Plan is, if you will simply practice this Technique faithfully and will keep "asking" for the inner leading. It will come. And be ready, when it does, to follow your Good Motivations. Do joyously all the good things you feel motivated to do in your daily life. Nothing and no one should stop your doing GOOD!

After you have mastered the Basic Technique of Light, begin to make constant use of the following:

THE NEW AGE BALANCE TECHNIQUE

Step 1. Close your eyes and let yourself relax. Now picture in your mind a large, brilliant Solar Sun. Fix your attention upon the exact center of that Sun.

Step 2. Mentally invite a single small ray of Pure White Light to come from the center of the Sun into you. See the ray of Pure White Light leaving the Sun and entering the center of your forehead. Will that the Light (that spiritual Light) shall enter the exact center of your Pituitary Gland, which is situated directly back of the eyes at the approximate center of your head.

Step 3. Now speak these words: "Let the Christ in the Sun (Son) balance me (or another person) NOW!"

When using this for another, you must send the ray of Pure White Light from the center of your forehead into the "Balance Center" or Pituitary Gland of the other person. All that is required to do this is for you to make a vivid contact with the Solar Sun by forming a clear mental image of it in your own mind. Your ability to "balance" yourself and others will grow with much practice. Keep trying until results indicate you have proven the technique works perfectly. Some persons do not show any results until after several "try's". Others are amazed at instantaneous proof and benefits.

Only good can possibly come from use of this Technique and the benefits -- instant rebalancing of the entire body from head to toe, left to right, front to back and perfect alignment with the all-pervading Life Force -- are beyond all monetary price. It is one of the priceless gifts to Humanity entrusted now to you to use for the restoring of lost Harmony and Balance on this Planet.

YOUR SPECIAL INSTRUCTIONS NOW

1. USE THE TECHNIQUE OF LIGHT DAILY. Practice drawing Cosmic Light Power into your body 3 minutes or more each day. Send the Power out to bless and heal other persons.

2. USE THE BALANCE TECHNIQUE NOW. Don't miss a single day of practicing this marvelous Technique. It is simply a "must" for all New Agers who desire a higher, more positive level of Health, Harmony and Happiness for Mankind.

3. RADIATE LIFE, LOVE AND LIGHT. Send out "New Age" Thought Forms of Life, Love and Light as you go about your daily chores. Make your Thoughts stronger than ever before. How? By filling them with the vitalizing Christ-Balance Light. Vigorous "New Age" thoughts will counteract and dissolve negative thought forms around you and help us all hold the balance for HARMONY AND PEACE on Planet Shan..NOW.

4. BE A SHEPHERD TO YOUR FELLOWMAN. Step forth boldly and speak the New Age "Word" to everyone who will listen. But still more important, demonstrate the great practical value and wisdom of this by becoming a Tower of Shining Strength.

The New Age Message must go forth to groups, individuals and to distant places of this globe. This will help to foster the spirit of good will and mutual understanding, for, as said by one Edgar Dodd of England,"most problems have their origin in the individual, but have a reflection in world affairs". Our motto is: "EACH ONE REACH ONE!" with the Message!

Of course, as soon as the great import of the New Age Message hits you...I doubt if you will remain content just to reach only ONE person. You will go "all out". That is why the mental level is so vital. Until you really understand the Message yourself, your efforts at passing the word to others will be feeble. But if you do study to know more about the New Age pattern and what the closely impending Golden Age means to all Humanity...I venture to say your work will become tremendously IMPORTANT.

YOUR PART IN THE GREAT PLAN

Part 4

Aid From Outer Space

What part do the mysterious objects in our skies -- the UFO's or unidentified flying objects -- have in this Great Plan? Are they here to help, confuse, or hinder?

I believe "they" are in our skies to serve us, and to serve The Great Plan of God.

How serve us? Not by making mass "public appearances" which would frighten the wits out of men, women and children here on Earth. Not that way. At least, up to this point, that has not been their approach.

They come to help all of us Earthlings "awaken" mentally and spiritually. To what? I think you have already guessed the answer. They want us to awaken and realize that a Cosmic Drama -- big and bold and beautiful -- is unfolding right under our very noses.

The Great Plan -- Space Phase -- is in operation. The advanced beings of other worlds have been trying to alert us Earthlings to the fact that interplanetary life is not a dream -- but real -- and Space Visitors to Earth are real.

Of course it all ties in with The Great Plan. A big change in vibration is due for Planet Earth, and for all other planets in this Solar System.

"They" have and are still endeavoring to aid Mankind on Earth by appearing in our skies and by contacting many of us mentally and telling us to "wake up" and "prepare!"

Prepare for what? For the changes ahead. For the increase of Solar Light vibrations as the Golden Age draws nearer and nearer. Prepare mentally, physically, and most vitally of all, prepare spiritually!

I've been in the New Age work for more than ten years. I have personally seen and contacted -- to my complete satisfaction -- "Flying Saucers" or craft from outer space origins, on several occasions. Spaceships from other dimensional worlds, from other planets beyond the Earth, are to me no mere whim or fancy. I know they are real. You, most likely, have had one or more "sightings" yourself.

I don't need to convince you. Friend to friend, I doubt if anything I could say would really persuade you on the subject unless you had some experiences of your own.

But I shall assume you are a believer in the existence and actuality of UFO's. Your mind, at any rate, is open. Bless you! Not everyone I meet is open-minded.

You might like to hear a little story. It's a true one. One day I sent out some notices regarding my book titled: FLYING SAUCER REVELATIONS, to a new mailing list. Orders for the book came pouring in and of course this made us happy. But one fellow did not order. He just wrote a "note" to me on the back of the Order Form, saying:

"MICHAEL X. Dear Sir: There are no flying saucers. I will give twenty-five dollars to any person showing me a flying saucer. You are a fake and a liar. I have already read books about "flying saucers" and they were BUNK.!!!! Can't you make an honest living without fooling people? You will not get any money from ME!"

For some strange reason he forgot to sign the note. I wonder if he thought I might just turn the tables on him and point out a real flying saucer to him sometime? If that happened, not only would he be out $25.00. He'd also have to change his whole "frame of reference" of thinking!

Actually, the really vital thing is not a question of whether Spaceships from other worlds exist. It is what they signify, what they mean to us that is so important.

What do they signify? Mastery. That is what they signify. Those souls who come in Spaceships from other worlds are Enlightened Ones. They've taken "One Step Beyond" the unawakened Human state wherein Man feeds only his "little Ego" or personal self. They have passed over into the Enlightened Sector of Being wherein they love and serve the "great Self" or Divine Self in all Humanity. Selfish? No. Nor dangerous.

Now let's ask another big question. Will positive aid come from outer space to you when you serve the Great Plan? Absolutely! Undoubtedly, YES! Tremendous aid, assistance,

direction will be given to you from outer space, by the
Space People who are working with The Plan. Remember, it
is a mighty Plan for Good...Universal Good...and essentially
it is Our Creator's Plan for Man's evolutionary "upgrading".

This upgrading will work out without fail, because it
is not dependent upon any human will at all. It is a Cosmic
Event. A recurring Event. The recurrence in our Solar System
of another "Golden Age" of shining glory for all beings on
Planet Earth...after 7200 years of waiting!

The aid will be given to you from higher thought realms,
by "Telethot" reception. It will be practical aid, in that
the thoughts you will pick up from now on will be providing
great "boosting power" to your mind and soul.

That, by the way, is the way you can be sure that your
aid is really coming from desirable high sources. It will
deal directly with the expanding of your three Divine functions which are these:

1. You function as PROPHET (your soul-mind interprets
                                   The Plan)
2.   "   "   " PRIEST (you teach, uplift, bless)
3.   "   "   " KING   (you personally manage your
                    or QUEEN (self and activities so that
                                   (you rise above "little self"
                                   (& live from Christ-Awareness.

I do not doubt that a clearer picture--much clearer than
the one I am bringing to you here--will be revealed to you
regarding The Great Plan. My job is simply to open the door
enough for you to catch the vision. Then those who are actively working on the higher planes right now will carry on
from that point and "fill in" the details.

Your job is to "attune" yourself with The Plan...with
the Purpose of it all. How exactly, may you know if you are
really "in tune" with The Plan?

That's easy to determine. If you have lost interest in
your fellow Earthlings and your own soul-progress you are
out of tune with The Plan. To be out of harmony with the
Divine Star in our brother is to be out of harmony with God.

Any time we are out of harmony with our Maker we are
not in attunement with The Great Plan. After all, it is
God's Plan for Man. And of course, if we get out of attunement with The Plan we are not in attunement with the Space
People because they are always in tune with God principles.

Part 5

"Rock Will Turn To Gold"

   At this very moment an ancient prophecy (one that is little known to our Western World) is coming true. I shall tell you about it in this chapter, for it will bring comfort and joy to you. I shall explain how.

   For the background of the prophecy we must travel now to Rome, Italy. Imagine that you are there with me; we are a couple of happy "touristas".

   There is much of interest to see in Rome, and as we pass by the various shops in the business district we note with a thrill that there is "never a dull moment" in Rome. Always something happening. And the people are very expressive. If something pleases them they let everyone know about it. And if something disturbs them they let you know about that, too.

   Oh, oh. What is this? We've reached the City Square and for some strange reason we are attracted toward one of the large statues that stands there. The statue is old, and it is of some nobleman of the royal Italian family. At the base of this statue we see a plaque. It says:

   "When the Rock turns to Gold, the end of the world will come." What a strange prophecy! You look at me for some kind of a reasonable interpretation. I smile back at you, but I don't give any interpretation. You see, the prophecy has startled me just as much as it has you. And I cannot, at the moment, shed much light upon it.

   We continue our "sightseeing" of Rome. But after the impact of having come face to face with one of the most unusual and bewildering predictions we've seen for a long time, none of the other sights hold much interest for us.

   That night we have Dinner together at one of the quaint cafes that you took such a fancy to earlier in the day. I give orders to the waiter for an interesting meal and suddenly you say:

"MICHAEL X, I can't get that strange prophecy out of my mind. What does it mean? It must have some meaning!"

Then, like a bolt of lightning out of the blue, the answer flashes across my mind. I lean toward you, close so that every word will register clearly in your consciousness. Your eyes are gleaming in the soft light of the cafe.

"When the Rock turns to Gold," I reply with a deep current of emotion running through the tones of my voice, "refers to the planet Earth or "Rock" coming into the New Age vibration; the highly stepped-up light frequency from the Central Sun Vela. When that happens, our Earth will turn to Gold...that is, this Golden Age vibration will turn the planet into Gold, which signifies "Spiritual Awareness".

Earth Matter being changed -- lifted into a NEW state of vibration -- Golden Age vibration! That was it!

Your eyes beam approval, recognition. And I continue.

"The end of the world will come." This does not mean the end of our planet nor of its usefulness to Mankind. It refers only to the "end of an Age, or cycle". We've come to the closing days of the Old Era, or Old Dispensation as of now. We are living in the Harvest Time of the Latter Days which prophets have been predicting for centuries!"

You nod and I sense you are in full agreement with the interpretation of the prophecy. In comes the Italian waiter and our spirits perk up at the sight of a pair of delicious looking fresh green salads.

"I am still not clear on one thing," you confess in deep sincerity and frankness.

"What is that?"

"How do I fit into the Golden Age picture? I mean, what is the use of my knowing all about the coming of the stronger Light vibrations from Vela if there is nothing I can do to help out the general situation somehow? I feel this change is going to affect people everywhere and may cause confusion.

"That's just it," I reply. "It is part of your Special task to help prevent panic and fear on this planet Earth.. now and more especially in the critical days ahead. Remember how years ago, the Orson Welles radio broadcast triggered a national panic when he announced over the air that Martians were invading the earth? Cold fear gripped America. People in 18 states committed suicide! No, you weren't told about that. But listen...

"We are living in the Last Days of the Old Era. Much will happen from now on to upset Mankind! UFO's (Unidentified Flying Objects) will play an increasing important role in "awakening" Earth people, during the Time of Turmoil ahead. Panic must be prevented. That is where you come in. Your NEW AGE knowledge and applied Techniques will help to stabilize, harmonize, and balance others in times of emergency. It is for this vital reason that you are asked to make every effort to master all Techniques given you!"

And I go on, "You are a New Age individual, my dear friend. Out of the confusion, turmoil and chaos of these closing days of the Old Era shall arise a nucleus of the NEW Humanity. The New Race of human beings shall arise. Though it may indeed seem strange for you to conceive at this time, The New Race shall consist of those souls who embraced The Plan. And though you may. not even realize it now, you are being prepared for the New Earth."

"Why me?"

"Because you are the kind of material needed by the Cosmic Architect of this Solar System. You are of the New Age calibre, and I'll tell you why I say this.

"First of all, you asked me a moment ago, how you could help out the general situation as the big change comes to the earth. This, in itself is one mark of a New Ager. There is a lot of love in you and you want to use that love constructively by loving the God-Self in others and in that practical way lift up your fellowmen. You've gone one step beyond personal self-love. I think you realize that whenever we try to use love selfishly we crush out ideals, start revolts, and wreck civilization! Secondly, you believe in non-violence."

For a long moment you say nothing. Then,

"Yes, Michael X, you are right about me. I do want to love rightly with everything that's in me. I do believe the New Age can come in without violence if harmonizing and balancing techniques are applied. I want to be of real service to others and to the Great Plan!

I look directly at you and reply quietly, "You shall."

I tell you that our strength as New Agers lies not in numbers but in purpose. Life is purpose and purpose is power.

I am counting on you to train yourself in Golden Age principles so that you become a LIGHT unto the whole world.

What is it that good men want? Isn't it simply to do good more effectively? And what is Good? According to one very wise friend of ours -- Aldous Huxley -- "Good is that which makes for Unity; Evil is that which makes for separateness." Our job then, is to unite all Mankind. How?

1. Each one of us must recognize the principle of "sharing". We share not only in the responsibility for what wrongs we've all done in the past -- the errors and misdemeanors that have accumulated in the present world confusion and chaos -- but we share in another way also. We share in educating all those who see the "Light" and are willing to work for Good.

2. For all those who have forgotten, we must emphasize the one big area of agreement on which we can meet all men. It is this: The divine fact that all men are related as brothers under the Fatherhood of God. A blood relationship exists between all men. Teach this fact and you dissolve racial barriers and end the spirit of "separateness" and hate in the world. No man shall enslave, dominate nor exploit another.

3. Foster the spirit of Goodwill and cooperation. By establishing this spirit more widely, so that it reaches the point of universality, New Agers will hold World Harmony.

4. Think, plan and act in terms of one life, one family, one humanity...regardless of race, color or background. One for all and all for one. The more we think in terms of oneness, instead of separateness, the quicker we shall banish "minority problems" and bring in the better life for all.

5. In whatever line of work you are now doing, be active for the good of the whole world. Help others to see and know that no man(as a man) is superior to another. Each evolves differently, developing unique qualities that are vitally needed.

It will help you greatly now if you will consciously pledge yourself to seek Divine Love, Life and Light. Know and realize that you are being watched over by beings who know more about The Great Plan and your part in it than you can possibly imagine. They are aiding you now.

THE MASTER PLAN is to build a new world, a balanced planet where the Christ Principle, perfect balance of Life, Love and Light in all beings reigns supreme. We are all deeply involved in this wonderful enterprise. Why not look in with me and see what other New Agers are doing now to serve the Great Plan?

YOUR PART IN THE GREAT PLAN

Part 6

"What Others Are Doing"

You have noticed the terrible unrest and confusion in the world today. It is the same old "Battle" of Light versus Darkness. Positive against Negative. Good versus Bad. Only today -- NOW -- the age-old battle between these two opposing forces is more disturbing and distressing.

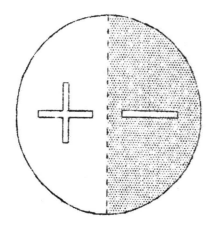

As the New Age enters, a strange thing will become more and more apparent. People in every walk of life will begin to perceive that the mobilizing of opposing forces is passe.

Instead, the object will be to establish an equilibrium of all forces -- within and without. Areas of agreement will be then sought by men whenever disputes of any kind arise between peoples. A universal "Equilibrium Law" will be discovered by "New Agers" who are in a position of authority and influence. And the former ways of the Old Era -- the tactics of "the General" will pass away into the Limbo of Forgotten Failures. Equilibration creates peace.

Impractical dreaming? By no means. We are talking now about the very same Universal Equilibrium Law that is at this precise moment, maintaining harmony, PEACE, and balance among all the stars, planets and suns in space.

Remember the New Age Balance Technique? It's that basic law of equilibrium applied to the individual. By practicing it exactly as instructed, you align your life (body, mind and emotions) to the Universal Equilibrium Law. And what happens? Plenty! Not only will this Balance Technique keep you in wonderful health...but also it will enable the God-Wisdom to flow more freely into your mind and soul. This will reveal to you -- from within yourself -- precisely what your part is in the scheme of things now! Poise brings truth.

Other NEW AGERS are doing it. They've learned the value, the priceless worth of the Technique. And New Age ideas and plans are pouring into their minds so fast they are absolutely

astounded. But it is all "in The Great Plan" and they
realize that. Nothing can hold them back from expressing
whatever talent or New Age aptitude they have.

Let me show you how good people everywhere are voluntarily cooperating with The Great Plan in a wonderful way.

One person I know -- we'll refer to her as Mary Jones
-- discovered that her part in The Plan right now was to
provide a meeting place in her home for "New Agers" to get
together. Nothing pleases her more than to help newcomers,
men and women who are attracted to New Age teachings, to
meet others in the movement. So, once each week she noti-
fies all the people on her mailing list, to come and enjoy
another friendly and enlightening "New Age Meeting".

I've spoken to her group on several occasions. When I
first had the privilege of talking before her group I found
only a mere "handful" of people there to listen to me. But
--and this is the important thing -- the last time I visited
the group there wasn't a vacant seat in the house! Not only
was there an abundance of people, but they were all the most
sincere and enthusiastic New Agers you'd ever want to meet.
Wonderful students. Hungry, yearning for TRUTH!

Another friend of mine found his "Special Role" in The
Golden Age Activity just in time. Just as he was about to
"retire" in 1944 (he'd reached retirement age) something
marvelous happened. He met Edgar Cayce, the famous clair-
voyant and healer, and was given a "Life Reading" by Edgar.

The Reading definitely instructed my friend to "Study
psychic gems and stones. Study them with the purpose of ac-
quainting individuals with them as well as preparing same."

Impressed? I'll say my friend was impressed. Without a
second's hesitation he immediately changed his plans for retirement and began to devote his time to the study of various
psychic gems -- such as the Lapis Lingua and the Telolith --
and out of that study grew a business known as "The Gem Ex-
change". Today, this individual is not only happy in his
"New Age work", but very busy and successful.

A New Ager who lives in Miami, Florida, found that his
particular "niche" in the Cosmic Plan was to receive thought
communications from advanced "space intelligences" in our
Solar System and relay those messages to other New Agers.
These messages, I might add, deal directly with the "Signs"
or "Marks" of this Old Era now closing. For that reason,
the identifying name of his work is "MARK-AGE".

Impending events, prophecies and a helpful interpretation of the unusual happenings in the world today are all part of the "MARK-AGE" program. It is helping many.

Here in California, an organization known simply as "UNDERSTANDING" is doing a fine work also. Local Units of this organization have sprung up in large and small cities all over this State, and the Group Leaders of the various Units are devotedly serving the cause of Truth. Their basic objective? To bring about "a better UNDERSTANDING between peoples of this world and an understanding of those not of this world!

Space-Age Clubs of all kinds and diverse names are established now in nearly all important cities of America. And not only in U.S.A. Canada is active in "New Age" work. England and other countries are doing their share.

How? By providing "meeting places" for New Agers...and it isn't important whether you happen to be "Seven or Seventy" years old. Chronological age means nothing in this movement. It's willingness to serve a big cause that is the important thing. Mankind must be awakened, inspired.

Lecturers on New Age subjects make the rounds of the various clubs regularly. A few years ago there were hardly enough public speakers to go around. Today there are many New Age Individuals who can talk easily and confidently before groups. And the "Good News" is spreading.

New Age Music is starting to "come into its own" too. A number of friends of mine are doing a great service for others by presenting "Golden Age Concerts" to the groups. These "Concerts" and "Symposiums" are tremendously effective in awakening the listeners on a "Soul Level" of response. For example, one excellent musician I know plays piano in a most extraordinary manner. It sounds more like "MUSIC OF THE SPHERES" and will certainly take you into "other dimensions" of Time and Space! He calls it VIBRASONIC MUSIC.
* * *
Yes, people everywhere are feeling the dynamic urge to align themselves positively to the Great Plan. None of us can wisely afford to stifle that God-given urge today!

"Behold! This is the Eternal Ordinance,
The Ordinance of Nature, Truth and Justice.
The Pure shall rise unto the Sun*
The impure...be forever clogged!**"
                                        Book of Enoch
*(Spiritual living)
**(Earthbound)

Part 7

Your Three Golden Keys

That wonderful Golden Age we are preparing for is not
-- I repeat emphatically -- NOT intended for the "laggards".
Laggards are those souls who are mentally backward, morally
backward, and ethically backward. Graduation day comes to

every school at the termination
of so many years of study. If
any student "lags" too far behind in his studies, he is not
permitted to enter the next higher grade in the school.

Let's compare this idea with
the idea of a major rise in vibration in our Solar System...
and a resulting CHANGED condition
of Planet Earth.

Those souls on Earth who are
in the "laggard" class are not
"prepared" mentally, morally, ethically, or"soul-wise" for
Golden Age living upon this New Earth. This situation is re-
solved by The Great Plan in a simple and reasonable way.

As the high, spiritual radiance from the Central Sun
Vela gradually increases its impact upon this Planet, the
laggards -- Spiritual slow-pokes -- on Earth will gradually
be taken out of physical embodiment. Those souls will not
return to Earth during the Golden Millenium. They will be
transported by Soul Guardians to another planet of an
equivalent vibration as Earth was before the Big Change.

Will their soul progress continue? Of course, but upon
another world in another region in space. And mercifully,
they will never remember ever having lived upon Earth.

Golden Ages do recur. But only once every 7200 years.
So if you and I happen to "miss the boat" this time.......?

But "missing the boat" is entirely unnecessary. Happily, there are THREE GOLDEN KEYS we may use now. These keys
are simple, definite, and intensely practical. They are giv-
en to you and other New Agers now in order that you may perform your individual part in the Plan successfully.

GOLDEN KEY #1. "RECEIVE FIRST!"

I fully believe that you, being a loyal New Ager, are generous, big-hearted and loving. You want to give your very best to others in loving service. But you cannot give successfully until you have first "received" something to give. So the practical rule is, receive first. You can't give out any more than you yourself have received.

Meditation -- that is, thinking about the Universal Source of Life, Love and Light -- is the Key to your New Age success. You are a living channel this moment for God's Life, Love and Light. "Connect up" to the main Power Station and increase your supply. Then you can really give.

Become the best "channel" possible, by observing five important steps. 1. Study Self; 2. Develop Self; 3. Forget Self and think of Purpose; 4. Keep yourself in balance and radiate your Life, Love and Light to the world. 5. Be ever watchful, vigilant, alert, that you do not fall back into the trap of the laggards who would hinder your upward progress. (Many, even the teachers, have fallen into that trap.)

Know that New Agers everywhere are working with you -- doing their part just as you are doing yours -- to bring enlightenment, joy and happiness to Mankind. You will most certainly fulfill your Special Role -- wider service to all Mankind in filling the special need that you alone can see and recognize to be your responsibility. Picture it clearly and begin now to act upon it with joyous effort each day.

And these New Age Techniques can help you. You can use the LIGHT TECHNIQUE AND THE BALANCE TECHNIQUE to draw into yourself more Power, Love and Wisdom. Then let that Power, Love and Widsom go forth for the upliftment of all.

GOLDEN KEY #2. "SELFLESS SERVICE"

You have passed "The Point of No Return" on the Path leading to the Stars when you realize within yourself that you can no longer live for yourself alone. A feeling of "Oneness with Humanity" has gripped you. Good! "One for all and all for one" is your Golden Motto.

But you cannot rest content inside yourself with just a good Motto. You now have a great urge to LIVE that Motto and help The Plan right where you are. So you start where you now are, using what you now have to work with (don't wait for better equipment) and do whatever you are impelled to do from within, to serve others. Whether you happen to be a plumber, a housewife, a professional person, garage mechanic -- no matter what you do for a livelihood -- you can serve more actively than before.

How? By expressing your "New Age Light" more actively. By radiating Life, Love and Light joyously because you know that your cause is just and your God is Good!

HELPING THE PLAN BY DISSOLVING NEGATIVITY.

You can help to dissolve the millions of negative and depressing thought forms that others -- especially the laggard souls -- have put into the atmosphere of this Planet Earth. Your thoughts can radiate such Good-Will, Harmony and Joy that they will at once "neutralize" and disintegrate the "Psychic Slough " of vicious thoughts that have been holding back Humanity's forward progress.

Each morning upon arising, do this. Raise your arms fully extended over your head, pointing toward the Sun. Take in Divine Power -- Life, Love, Light. Now lower your arms straight out in front of you. Spread fingers of both hands fanwise. Project the Divine Power to all living beings on this planet, animals as well as human beings.

GOLDEN KEY #3. "KEEP IT A SECRET!"

Whenever you are using the Light or Cosmic Life Energy to help others, be sure you do not at any time lay your hands upon their physical bodies. To do so would make you liable to the charge of "practicing healing without a Doctor's license." So it is wisest to observe this law. Do not lay hands upon anyone unless you are a Doctor or Minister who is legally qualified to do so.

Let your good work be a "Secret Service" to Humanity and for The Great Plan. Silence is power. Power to do is essential for your New Age activity. If this truth is realized you will never talk about your good works.

Your "left hand" will never know what your "right hand" is doing for the cause of Life, Love and Light on Earth. But YOU will know. The higher beings will know. And you will be contributing your due quota to The Plan by serving quietly without fanfare, or greater outer recognition.

Act as if you have "one essential task" to complete now. You have. It is to amplify the Golden Light for All.

MY NEW AGE PLEDGE

(NOTE: This Pledge is being made voluntarily now by the NEW AGERS everywhere. Will you join us in making the NEW AGE PLEDGE? All that is required is that you read the following paragraphs, slowly, thoughtfully and sincerely..MX)

1. I pledge myself now to be...A NEW AGE INDIVIDUAL.

2. I desire a higher, happier and nobler way of life. To attain this wonderful objective, I shall work with the Great Cosmic Plan. My outlook is now a Cosmic view. I look ever upward, onward and Godward (Goodward).

3. I shall energetically foster the Spirit of Good Will and Cooperation in my life and encourage it in the lives of others around me.

4. I refuse to let anything limit my opportunity to gain Cosmic Wisdom, Health and Freedom.

5. I fully recognize that I am now living in the Space Age and that interplanetary travel may soon become a fact for the people of Earth. I believe it is possible that intelligent human life now exists on other planets. It is entirely possible those human beings may be older, wiser, and more advanced in many ways than we are.

6. I am open-minded. Spacecraft of various kinds might very well be in use by other planetary beings who are more evolved than we are.

7. I have the "Spirit of Adventure"! I believe that my own thoughts have the power to bridge space -- that human intelligence can reach from planet to planet, from world to world, and that Mind-Power cannot be limited. I am not afraid of space. It is God's playground. I shall add power to my mind and to my soul each day. And I shall project my thought into the universe to uplift and bless all.

8. I am willing to serve the Great Plan. I am eager to be of genuine service to the One Universal Life, the One Universal Humanity, and the One Universal Creator. I see that service is more valuable than money. That money is only a symbol for service. To me, RIGHT ACTION is king. Right Action will always be action which serves The Great Plan. I am willing to serve it with head, heart and hand.

9. I am not afraid to face my Spiritual Destiny. What is
   my Destiny? To align myself rightly with the primary
forces of the Cosmos...LIFE, LOVE, LIGHT. To balance the
negative and positive forces within myself by using the New
Age Balance Technique faithfully. I know that by so doing,
I shall grow ever wiser and expand into FREEDOM.

10. I pledge myself to make every effort to transmute my
    lower nature -- the Old Age Man -- into the Higher Self.
I shall retain all that is useful and inspiring and shall
discard the old and unnecessary. I can do this without re-
sistance and struggle, for I welcome the new and better ways
and I see the old ways falling away like husks, discarded.
In this way I proceed along the High Path leading to the
stars. I will build upon those things of true value, refus-
ing to give attention to things not of true value. But I
will never cease my search for NEW KEYS, NEW PRINCIPLES that
may enable me -- and my fellowman -- to live more harmoniously.

11. I believe that the highest religion is to do good with
    all my might, by cooperating with the Universal Life,
Love and Light everywhere. I pledge myself to serve the One
Life which is everywhere, and the One Humanity. And to as-
sist it to unfold itself into higher expressions.

12. I shall put the greatest emphasis upon "learning HOW to
    LIVE" more healthfully, happily and nobly..rather than
upon "getting a living" or "amassing great wealth". To me
the art and science of LIVING SPIRITUALLY comes first. The
business of getting a living is second, important tho' it be.

13. I pledge myself to seek in receptive silence for a
    clear and definite leading..as to MY PART in the Mighty
Plan for Good that is now unfolding itself. Whatever Part
is given me in The Creator's Plan, I accept joyously and with
appreciation. I shall do my part unstintingly. I realize
that cooperation with others is necessary for the success of
The Plan. I know that Cooperative Brotherhood, under God,
is the Way of Love -- and I choose the Way of Love.

                    SO MOTE IT BE -- SELAH

                    * * * * * * *

Dear New-Age Friend:

     I leave you now with this Benediction. May you
enter freely into Cosmic Love, the state of Perfect
Order, Balance and Harmony. May you bring forth increasing "Good Works" that uplift the whole world.
May you unfold gloriously the CHRISTED SELF within!

                              MICHAEL X

THE GREAT INVOCATION

From the point of Light within the Mind of God,
Let Light stream forth into the minds of men.
Let Light descend on Earth.

From the point of Love within the Heart of God,
Let Love stream forth into the hearts of men.
May Christ* return to Earth.

From the centre where the Will of God is known,
Let purpose guide the little wills of men --
The purpose which the Masters know and serve.

From the center which we call the race of men,
Let the PLAN of Love and Light work out.
And may it seal the door where evil dwells.

Let Light and Love and Power restore the PLAN
                                        on Earth!
*(God in Man)

* * * * * * *

THE SECOND INVOCATION

Let the Lord of Liberation issue forth;
Let Him bring aid to the Sons of men.
Let the Rider from the Secret Place come forth
And coming, save.

Let the souls of men awaken to the Light, and
May they stand with massed intent.

Let the Fiat of the Lord go forth!
The end of woe has come --
Come forth O mighty one!

The hour of service of the Saving Grace
Has now arrived.
Let it be spread abroad, O Mighty One!
The Rule of evil now must end!

AFTERWORD

In the "It Can Now Be Told" Department, we may now reveal that the spaceman who contacted Michael X. Barton was none other than the enlightened Venusian thinker, Valiant Thor. Unfortunately, this sleight-of-hand was necessary at the time, due to heightened Cold War tensions and various threats that had been made against Thor and his family, who were working hard to end nuclear bomb testing on Earth. Since Barton was a popular New Age personality in the Los Angeles area, it was crucial that he be among the first Earthlings contacted.

Barton's contacts came prior to Valiant Thor's forced internment in the Pentagon between 1957 and 1960, after which the Thor family became more circumspect about working with citizens of our planet. As such, this book is a bit of a time capsule, highlighting the warm, helpful feelings that Venusians once had for Earthlings. Thor, in particular, is known for having worked closely with Nikola Tesla, sharing all the knowledge he could with that advanced human, even though some of it may have skirted the fringes of galaxial law (which states that we should merely observe underdeveloped species, rather than actively intervene on their behalf).

As we reprint many of the books that we first published many years ago, it should become obvious that Valiant Thor was never totally imprisoned in the Pentagon. As mentioned in Dr. Frank E. Stranges' "Stranger at the Pentagon," Thor could sneak out anytime he wanted. And he did so many times, in order to spread, to various contactees, the anti-nuclear message that was so important then - as it is now.

Luckily, Thor succeeded, and was able to convince world leaders to pull back from the abyss of all-out nuclear war. Unfortunately, his good friends John F. Kennedy, Martin Luther King, and Robert F. Kennedy were all assassinated, setting us back greatly in our efforts to become an enlightened society. We are still struggling with the forces of ignorance and intolerance today.

The work of Valiant Thor and his Venusian associates

was obviously of great importance in helping mankind through a difficult time. What we will ultimately do with the many concepts that Thor gifted Tesla, Barton, and others is, of course, still up in the air. But, so far, so good.

I ask my readers now to continue supporting the endeavors of these courageous Venusians, and their Great Plan. May we all someday experience a world free of fear and war, and enjoy our birthright as free citizens of this galaxy.

-Gray Barker, 1982

16841012R00022

Made in the USA
Middletown, DE
26 November 2018